Meditations on Humility

St. Francis Borgia

MEDITATIONS ON HUMILITY

And Other Reflections

SOPHIA INSTITUTE PRESS
Manchester, New Hampshire

Original edition: *Spiritual Works of Saint Francis Borgia*
(London: Thomas Richardson and Sons, 1875).

Slight alterations have been made in this text to
make it more accessible to modern readers.

Cover design by LUCAS Art & Design, Jenison, MI.

On the cover: cross courtesy of Pixabay (ai-
generated-9115803_1920.png).

Unless otherwise noted, Scripture quotations are taken from
the Douay-Rheims edition of the Old and New Testaments.

Sophia Institute Press
Box 5284, Manchester, NH 03108
1-800-888-9344
www.SophiaInstitute.com

paperback ISBN 979-8-88911-567-0
ebook 979-8-88911-568-7

Library of Congress Control Number: 2025937006

First printing

Contents

Reflections for Holy Communion

Daily Reflections for Greater Self-Knowledge

Preface

St. Francis Borgia was preparing himself to leave the world and join the Society of Jesus when he composed, in his retreat at Gandia, the following little treatises. He wrote them for his own direction, not thinking that they would be beneficial to others besides himself. But God did not permit that the lights which He had communicated to His servant should be long hidden. The writings of the Duke of Gandia were published at Salamanca by the celebrated Dr. Michel de Torrès, who later became himself one of the lights of the Society of Jesus in Spain. From Salamanca, these writings spread in a very short time through all the towns of Spain. They were translated into different languages and everywhere produced admirable fruits of grace. But that which ought to make us esteem them most is that they have been the means by which God has been pleased to raise St. Francis Borgia to that eminent sanctity that makes him venerated throughout the world. In them can be clearly seen the character of his virtue, and that spirit of penitence and humility by which he was led, and that he preserved to the end of his life. These pages, written by a saint, have, in their simplicity, a divine eloquence. Through them the Duke of Gandia confides to us his inmost thoughts. We hear the favorite of Charles V, at the highest point of fortune, proving in his own person that all which is not eternal is nothing and that there is no true greatness in the world but in serving God. These pages have not ceased, during three centuries, to elevate and fortify souls; they have detached them from time and prepared them for eternity. It is to perpetuate their apostleship that we offer them anew to the public.

Introduction

What is the greatest weapon in the spiritual life? Is it fasting on bread and water? Praying the Rosary? Frequenting the Sacraments? All play a crucial role in defeating Satan, but one wields tremendous power—humility. Pride led to Satan's downfall, while humility lifted the saints to glory. Satan is no match for a truly humble soul. Humility is the virtue whereby we see ourselves as God sees us, which leads us to give Him all glory and honor.

Satan hates humility because this virtue is an icon of Jesus, who said, "Take up my yoke upon you, and learn of me, because I am meek, and humble of heart: and you shall find rest to your souls" (Matt. 11:29). Humility also reminds Satan of Our Lady, who proclaimed, "My soul doth magnify the Lord. And my spirit hath rejoiced in

God my Saviour" (Luke 1:46–47). Thus, humility is the face and heart of Jesus and Mary, the foundation of all virtues. It unlocks the gates of Heaven, for every saint was truly humble.

When asked about the three most important virtues, many saints would reply, "humility, humility, and humility." Acquiring this virtue takes a lifetime of struggle—blood, sweat, tears, humiliations, and above all, grace.

Throughout Church history, God has raised up saints to teach us how to pray and grow in virtue. One such saint was St. Francis Borgia. Born in 1510 as the son of a Spanish Duke, he had every reason for pride—titles, wealth, intelligence, and a dignified appearance. He was the great-grandson of both Pope Alexander VI, and King Ferdinand II of Aragon.

Yet, St. Francis Borgia spent his life conquering pride and striving to imitate Jesus through humility, as he wrote in *Meditations on Humility*:

> It is certain that the principal cause of pride, and of all inordinate desire for worldly greatness, comes from the vain esteem we have of ourselves, which the enemy of our salvation tries evermore to increase by filling our minds with a countless

> number of vain imaginings that prevent us knowing the truth and make us conceal from ourselves our real state.

As a devoted husband and father of eight, St. Francis Borgia lived a godly marriage until the unexpected loss of his wife. After ensuring his children were cared for, he joined the Society of Jesus (Jesuits). A friend of St. Ignatius of Loyola and Fr. Peter Faber, S.J., he was later elected the third Superior General of the Jesuit Order. During his seven-year leadership, he focused on revising Jesuit rules, expanding missions in India and the Americas, and guiding the Society's growth.

Often overlooked is that St. Francis Borgia was also an exorcist—one of the greatest of his time. He faced the devil directly and overcame him through the power of humility. His life and words in this important book offer valuable guidance for resisting evil and deepening prayer. Clearly, St. Francis Borgia's wisdom and life plan led him to great holiness, first as a married man and later as a religious priest.

Like St. Ignatius of Loyola's Spiritual Exercises, which continue to guide countless souls in discernment and a deeper love for God, *Meditations on Humility* can similarly draw souls closer to Christ Crucified through meditation on Jesus' humility. As St. Francis Borgia wrote, "When you are answered with contempt and treated with disrespect—think of the indignity with which our Savior was treated in the house of Caiphas."

Humility is the greatest weapon in the spiritual life, enabling a soul to conquer Satan, resist evil, and advance toward sainthood. These inspiring pages offer a firsthand glimpse into St. Francis Borgia's spirituality and heroic virtue as you allow him to become your spiritual master on the path to humility.

—Patrick O'Hearn

Meditations on Humility

The Remedy against Pride

It is easy to know, from the misfortunes that pride has caused in Heaven and on earth, what are the advantages of humility. The Holy Scriptures and the Fathers speak so much in praise of this virtue because its practice is necessary for a spiritual life and because it is the basis and foundation of all Christian perfection. Certainly, it would avail us nothing to have acquired knowledge, fortitude, charity, and all the other virtues if they were not accompanied by humility. For, in a word, of what use is almsgiving if void of humility and full of vainglory? What advantages will those who are esteemed brave and valiant draw from their brilliant actions if they are not humble? The same can be said of all the other virtues. The sad consequences of pride are known to everybody. It has precipitated rebellious angels from the glory of Heaven into the depths of Hell; it has deprived man of that happy state of justice and innocence in which he had been created. But as I do not intend to speak here of the necessity and advantages of humility, without which all our actions, however holy they appear in the eyes of men, are abominable before God, I shall only propose the means of acquiring a virtue so excellent and so necessary.

Persuade yourself, then, my dear reader, that the enemies of your salvation use so many artifices to deprive you of this precious treasure because, without extreme vigilance, you will at any moment be in danger of losing it. Prepare yourself, then, carefully against the surprises of pride, and learn the way to combat so formidable an enemy. For if you preserve humility of heart, you will also easily preserve innocence, since the Scriptures tell us that God gives grace to the humble and resists the proud: "In like manner, ye young men, be subject to the ancients. And do you all insinuate humility one to another, for God resisteth the proud, but to the humble he giveth grace" (1 Pet. 5:5).

Finally, it should be sufficient to give you a love for this virtue to consider that the ever Blessed Virgin, although she was enriched with all the gifts of Heaven, only spoke of her humility when she wished to glorify the Lord—"he hath regarded the humility of his handmaid" (Luke 1:48)—and that the Savior of the world recommends us above all things to learn from Him mildness and humility (see Matt. 11:29).

It is certain that the principal cause of pride, and of all inordinate desire for worldly greatness, comes from the vain esteem we have of ourselves, which the enemy of our salvation tries evermore to increase by filling our minds with a countless number of vain imaginings that prevent us from knowing the truth and make us conceal from ourselves our real state. Thus, to cure us of so dangerous a blindness, it is necessary to apply the contrary remedies and to fill our minds with all that is capable of making us know our own nothingness and of inspiring us with the true ideas we ought to have of ourselves. And as pride is a poison infinitely subtle and insinuates itself everywhere, even into our most saintly actions, it is doubly necessary to use every means to combat it. You should employ yourself in reflecting upon God, upon creatures, upon things spiritual and corporal, interior and exterior. In order to do so with advantage, this little treatise is divided into three parts that will teach you the way to humble and confound yourself: first, by the consideration of the things that are below the earth; second, by the consideration of those that are on the earth; and third, and lastly, by the consideration of those that are above us, such as the angels, the saints, and God Himself. I hope that all who apply themselves to this exercise will soon become humble before God, with the help of His holy grace.

Part I

Considering the Things Below the Earth

There are several things in Hell whose consideration is incalculably capable of keeping down the swellings of pride, of filling us with humility, and of making us know the abyss of our nothingness; for it must be acknowledged that it is a great subject of humiliation for us that the devils were damned to eternal torments for one single sin while we have not been condemned to Hell after having committed so many.

And we, who have offended the Divine Majesty oftener and more grievously than the angels, are so ungrateful that we do not repent, although God, in His mercy, gives us time.

Reflecting on the Reality of the Devil, Demons, and the Damned

We do not read that Lucifer used so many artifices to draw his accomplices in his sin, as it is the custom for men to do to draw their fellow men into it. For men are not content with simply putting before their eyes the occasions of sin, as Lucifer did: they beg, they entreat, they employ their riches, they sometimes even hazard their life and their honor for this purpose.

Truly, this ought to humble us exceedingly, and our humility should be followed by a sorrow and repentance capable of delivering us from the eternal shame that is prepared for us in Hell in punishment of such wickedness. This is the more evident as, by our vicious habits and by the sad inclination that we have to evil, we invite in some manner the devil to tempt us, and we help him ourselves to make us fall into sin. This is why so many deceive themselves, who attribute to temptation the disorders of their lives, although they are themselves the principal authors of their ruin, having drawn on the devil to destroy them. Thus, they should consider themselves to be the more guilty; and, as great criminals are full of shame and sadness when they appear in the midst of their accomplices before the judges of this world, sinners should also appear, in this state, before the tribunal of the Sovereign Judge, surrounded by the demons, their accomplices in their crimes.

If the sinner ponders on all these things attentively, it will be easy for him to recognize what great reason he has for humbling himself and for confessing before God that he has deserved to suffer the greatest punishment, not only in time but still more in eternity. So that were he doomed to bear in this life all the torments and ignominy that could be endured, he ought to be convinced that this would be very little in comparison with what he has deserved to suffer in Hell. Let him, then, abase himself before his Lord, confess his own misery, and ask mercy from God, while recognizing himself, nevertheless, unworthy of obtaining it.

But as there are some persons who, finding themselves free from the irregularities of which I have spoken, may perhaps persuade themselves that they have no occasion to humiliate themselves before God, I believe I am bound to undeceive them as to so gross an error by praying them to consider that no person can assert he is perfect and that those who believe themselves virtuous, and whom everybody esteems saints, have the more reason to be ashamed of themselves. For it is certain that there is not a moment in which God does not deliver them from Hell by His preserving grace, without which they would fall at once into sin and make themselves worthy of eternal torments.

Is it not, then, only just that we should return our Lord unceasing thanks for so great a benefit, and that we should annihilate ourselves before Him and consider that not only are we unworthy of so much mercy but are even quite incapable of thanking Him for it? Hence, if each one of us will reflect on what obligation he would owe to anyone who had delivered him from Hell after he had fallen into it, he will understand that he owes no less to God who has kept him from it by the preserving power of His grace. If we would often occupy ourselves with these thoughts, and with the thanksgiving that we owe to God for so inestimable a favor, we would feel, without doubt, our hearts penetrated with a saving confusion, and this confusion would be followed by an interior peace and consolation that the world cannot give. For God loves, above all things, the praises of a contrite and humble heart, according to the words of the prophet: "He hath had regard to the prayer of the humble: and he hath not despised their petition" (Ps. 101:18); "To my hearing thou shalt give joy and gladness: and the bones that have been humbled shall rejoice" (Ps. 50:10).

Truly, if we find matter for self-abasement in the thought of the demons, how much more ought we to find in the thought of human beings that are damned? I am well aware that we are told with reference to the rebel angel that because he was a spirit there was no time of mercy given to him after the first sin. But what can be said of men to whom it has availed nothing for salvation to have been formed of earth and to have had so weak and frail a body of flesh? For, in short, are there not many who, after the commission of their first mortal sin, were buried in Hell?

Alas! Alas! The sinner who considers the enormity of his crimes, who knows how easy it is to fall at any moment into sin, and who sees how many less weak than himself have been damned forever for having fallen but once, should indeed tremble for himself! For if those who committed but one sin have merited the eternal punishment of Hell, what will those deserve who have committed many?

Let such try, then, sincerely to humble themselves, and let them consider, for their still greater humility, that if they are not burning at this moment in unquenchable flames, they owe it alone to the mercy of God, and not to any merit of their own.

Reflecting on Limbo and Purgatory

We can, in the second place, derive much profit by meditating on Limbo[1]—a great subject for humiliation before God—by reflecting on the grace with which He has preserved us, ourselves and the mothers who bore us, since our conception up to our Baptism, from the numberless dangerous accidents to which our lives were exposed. Let us weep, then, for our ingratitude in not thanking God

[1] Limbo is a theological hypothesis or theory about what happens to unbaptized, good people when they die, especially unbaptized infants. It both admits the limitations of what salvation we can achieve without the grace of Baptism (the ordinary means of being cleansed from Original Sin) and considers that a good and loving God would not simply leave those souls in Hell who are innocent of personal sin. Limbo is not a doctrine of the Church and was specifically relegated as a hypothesis by the International Theological Commission, under Pope Benedict XVI, in 2007. On the other hand, the Church officially teaches the reality of Purgatory as doctrine: "All who die in God's grace and friendship, but still imperfectly purified, are indeed assured of their eternal salvation; but after death they undergo purification, so as to achieve the holiness necessary to enter the joy of Heaven. The Church gives the name Purgatory to this final purification of the elect" (*Catechism of the Catholic Church*, 1030–1031).

for so great a blessing; for the souls in Limbo have never offended God, and we, by offending Him, frequently deserve to be in Hell, which is a place much darker and deeper than Limbo. These poor souls are below the earth, although they are without sin, and we who are so sinful are above them. Alas! If they are deprived of the sight of God, all innocent as they are, how can such criminals as we dare to look at them? Indeed, if we compare their deficiencies with our own, we shall feel so much shame that we shall not even dare to raise our eyes toward Heaven.

But the thought of Purgatory, and of those faithful souls who are there, satisfying the Divine Justice, is still more capable of lowering our self-esteem. They are secure against the temptations of the world and the occasions of sin, because they are already arrived in port; instead of being, as we are, still in the midst of the sea, exposed to the tempest, uncertain of our salvation, and surrounded by numerous and very formidable enemies. If they endure such great pain, although they are already in a place of safety, what ought not we to suffer who live amidst so many dangers? But if the contemplation of what they suffer for their own imperfections is not capable of humbling us, let us reflect on how we have added to their torments; in the case of some, because they followed the bad example and pernicious counsel we gave them; in that of others, on account of the little care we took to correct them when they were with us on earth, a care we could easily have taken; and, finally, in the case of not a few, on account of our hard-heartedness and negligence in not relieving them by our prayers and alms. Let us humble ourselves, then, in considering how we have increased the pain these souls endure and how we have neglected to deliver them from it. Let us think how much greater our faults are than theirs, and that we, perhaps, will never be judged worthy of expiating them in Purgatory.

Part II

Considering the Things on the Earth

What sentiments ought we to have of ourselves at the sight of creatures who have never sinned, having already judged ourselves more guilty than those who are rebels and whom God punishes with so much rigor? These creatures that have never sinned are inanimate and deprived of reason, but they have never strayed in anything from the order of their Creator. What a subject for shame, then, has man in his disobedience, since he alone, of all creatures, has overthrown the order that God has established! And the better to understand all the reasons we have for humbling ourselves, let us cast our eyes on all the creatures that surround us.

What Nature Teaches Us About Humility

Let us consider that the earth is naturally prolific in producing all kinds of fruit, and that we are sterile by nature and incapable of performing any good work. Let us remember that the water has been given to us to fertilize the earth and to quench our thirst, and that we have refused it to God, from whom we received it, in refusing it to the poor who ask for a drink in the name of God.

Let us consider that the fire that warms us and prepares the food that nourishes us in this life shall perhaps be our punishment in the next; that this same fire, which appears to us so intense, is nothing in comparison to that which the anger of God has prepared for sinners.

Since the air we breathe unceasingly preserves our life, we are bound to employ it all in the service of Him who gave it, and it should be a great subject of humility for us if we have failed in doing so.

Let us reflect, with regard to the stones and rocks, that these were broken and rent at the death of our Blessed Savior, and that we are insensible at the sight of so much suffering.

Also, that the sweetness of honey should be changed into bitterness for us, who have made our Lord taste the insupportable bitterness of our crimes.

When we smell the perfume of flowers, let us think of the abominable stench of our sins.

Let us consider that the plants grow and shoot upward and that sinful man alone debases himself unceasingly by his attachment to terrestrial things. That we should imitate the luxuriant trees that strike their roots deep into the earth, that their branches may be loaded with fruit. Happy is the man who, in like manner, throws down deep roots of humility, that he may merit to produce abundant fruits of virtue!

Let us remember that we have rendered ourselves, by our sins, like the beasts that serve us; that they deserve less than ourselves to be ill-treated when they refuse to obey us, for they are deprived of reason; but we make use of the gifts of God to resist His will. God never repented having created the beasts, but He has repented of having created man. What a subject for humility for us!

If we accustom ourselves to consider the different instincts of animals, we shall constantly be able to gather from them many motives for humiliation. We can compare our little prudence in things that concern our salvation with that of the serpent, which puts one ear against the ground and covers the other with its tail for fear of hearing the voice of the charmer; and we can be confounded for so often listening to the temptations and deceits of the devil and the world.

On seeing the diligence with which the ant gathers together in the summer what will nourish it during winter, let us reflect that the time to provide those things that are necessary for us is passing rapidly, and that we are much to be pitied if we neglect to amass treasures of merit for the day of our death. But we should never end were we now to make reference to all that could humble us at the sight of creatures deprived of reason; and besides, those who wish to make themselves familiar with this exercise can easily find for themselves subjects for humility.

What Other People Teach Us About Humility

Let us proceed to consider reasonable creatures, that is to say, our brethren, who may be divided into three classes: namely, our superiors, our equals, or our inferiors. With regard to our superiors, it is sufficient to say that the power they have over us ought to make us humble and respectful toward them; and it would be foolish were we to act otherwise, knowing, as we do, whose place they hold on earth. Humble yourself, then, in thinking that, being the ministers of God, they have not treated you with the severity that you deserve for having so often revolted against Him. Thus, if they order you to do anything, if they blame you, or if they correct you, however hard the punishment may appear to others, it should to you appear light in comparison with what you deserve and with the infamous services that the devil exacts from you when your sins subject you to his tyranny. You would not at such time find any difficulty in being a murderer, either in deed or in thought. He makes you his miserable slave, working for him to throw into Hell the bodies and souls of those whom you drag into sin by your words and example. Certainly, if you consider how hard and shameful it is to serve so cruel a tyrant, it will appear infinitely sweet to see yourself engaged in the service of your legitimate Sovereign, who commands, above all things, mildness, peace, and union with your neighbor. Humble yourself, then, before the ministers of the divine power; and be well persuaded that you are unworthy to obey them while, nevertheless, you merit, when you render the obedience you owe them, to possess the eternal glory of Paradise.

To those who are your equals by their position, by their employment, or by their rank, humble yourself by acknowledging that you are unworthy of being their equal. Consider that you are, perhaps, much inferior to them in the sight of God; that you know your own sins, your own unruly desires and criminal thoughts; and that you cannot, without rashness, pass the same judgment upon others; consequently, you cannot be sure that you are equal to them, since it is certain that you are a sinner, and you are ignorant whether they are sinners.

When you see your neighbor ill, and you yourself are in good health, do not imagine that his illness is a punishment for his sins. Think, rather, that it is the effect of a particular love that God has for him, since He treats him in the same way as He treated His only Son. Think, too, that you are unworthy of such paternal correction, so full of tenderness and love. If, on the contrary, you are sick, and your neighbor is well in health, attribute your infirmity to your sins, which deserve a much more rigorous chastisement; and believe that he who is in health does not owe as much as you to the Divine Justice.

If you are rich, how these words of Jesus Christ should make you tremble: "Amen, I say to you, that a rich man shall hardly enter into the kingdom of heaven" (Matt. 19:23). When your neighbor possesses greater riches than yourself, conclude that he has made good use of the talent that the Lord has confided to him, and that he merits, by the good use he made of it, to have it increased.

If you are poor, attribute your poverty to a just judgment of God, who punishes you for having dissipated the spiritual gifts with which He had enriched your soul, or for having neglected to relieve the poor by your alms, or at least by your prayers. If your neighbor is in want, very far from esteeming him less, believe that God loads him with interior riches in order to render him entirely conformable to His well-beloved Son. Neither should you despise those who are below you; on the contrary, you ought to respect them, since you see that the providence of God more frequently makes use of persons contemptible in the eyes of the world, for the accomplishment of His designs, than of those who hold the first rank. If God has placed you in a high position, do not attribute it to your own merit. Persuade yourself rather that He has had compassion on your weakness; that He has wished to spare you; that you are not suited to a laborious life; that you have not strength of mind enough to support great adversities; and that you would undoubtedly have sunk under the hardships borne by those whom the necessities of their condition oblige to work day and night for the sustenance of their life.

If you have servants, humble yourself at seeing that they obey, serve, and honor you, although you have often refused to obey your Sovereign Lord, and to render Him the honor and services which you owe Him. In the end, you will never be at a loss for reasons for humbling yourself at the sight of any person, however contemptible he may appear to you, if you reflect that he is the work of the hand of God, made in His own image, and that the Eternal Father has loved all men, even to abandoning His only Son to the death of the Cross to give them life.

What Those Outside the Faith Teach Us About Humility

Even infidels[2] may offer us a subject of humility. Jesus Christ died for them as well as for us; they were created in the image of God like ourselves. It is true that they are not illuminated with the light of faith and that they are deprived of the consolation that they taste who are in the service of the true God, but it is this very thing that should confound us: for they undergo the greatest labors and subject themselves to the most rigorous fasts in honor of the false divinities whom they adore, and in order to

[2] "Infidels" here simply means those who are outside of the Christian Faith.

pay them a vain and superstitious worship. And we, who are Christians, enlightened with the purest lights of truth, fortified by the grace of the Holy Spirit, and animated with His love, we fail in courage when it is necessary for us to suffer anything for the honor of the true God, and for our own salvation. Humble yourself, then, at the sight of these unfortunate souls, and say to yourself: "If in Tyre and Sidon had been wrought the miracles that have been wrought in you, they had long ago done penance in sackcloth and ashes" (Matt. 11:21).

If you compare yourself with the Jews, you will again find matter for humility. It is true they crucified Jesus Christ; but they did it only once, and they did not recognize Him to be God. And you have many times crucified Christ by the sins you have committed, although you recognized Him perfectly and knew that He was the King of Glory, seated at the right hand of His Father.

What Our Fellow Christians Teach Us About Humility

But what shall I say of the humility you ought to have in considering Christians, who are much more perfect images of God than the rest of men, and whom the Holy

Scriptures do not hesitate to call gods: "I have said," cried the prophet, "you are gods and all of you the sons of the most High" (Ps. 81:6).

To conclude in a few words what remains to be said on this subject, I believe it will be very useful to keep ourselves in humility with regard to our neighbor, to reflect that the devil lays snares for us every instant to make us consent to pride, and that we shall undoubtedly fall into these snares if we are not extremely on our guard. Thus, every time we treat with our neighbor, we should observe ourselves carefully; have as much respect for him, whoever he be, as if he were our master or superior; listen to him when he speaks as if God were speaking by his mouth; value the good advice and wise instructions that he gives us; and, above all, take care not to think ourselves better than he, for fear of deceiving ourselves. For, besides being very bad judges of what we see, we allow ourselves frequently to be deceived by appearances, either by our want of discrimination or by the reserve of those with whom we treat. Thus, the surest means of not allowing ourselves to be mistaken in the judgments that we pass on our neighbor is to believe always that we may be deceived, to bless God for the good that we see in our brethren, ever to take the most favorable view of doubtful things, and not to condemn persons who seem to us to be wicked, since our duty is to judge ourselves only; on the contrary, we must charitably excuse them and consider that he whom we see do a bad action has before done numberless good ones; that if we compare ourselves to him, we shall have a greater subject for humility in our own faults than of scandal in his; that he has perhaps sinned through ignorance, or that he has already repented of his sin and is now in a state of grace; and above all, that his fall will perhaps procure for him in Heaven a higher degree of glory by the great penance that he has done for it.

You might also practice this exercise when speaking to others, with much spiritual advantage, by taking occasion to humble yourself in considering the subject-matter of your conversation. For example, when it turns upon mildness, think of the faults that anger has made you commit. When persons speak of beauty, think of the hideousness of your sins. When they speak of the power of the great in the world, consider that you are all weak and powerless as soon as there is question of undertaking anything for the glory of God, in spite of all your fixed resolves. When they speak of avarice, remember your irregularities and how you have dissipated the gifts of grace with which God had enriched you. Finally, if they speak of humility, cast your eyes on that secret pride that has made you commit so many great faults and corrupted your holiest actions. Thus, you will profit equally by the virtues and faults of your neighbor to preserve you in humility. The faults of others should make you remember your own, and their virtues should make you know how far you are from the perfection they have already attained. So that the conversation of men, which is usually the cause of so many sins, will become for you a source of grace and a school for humility.

Humility for Various Vocations and States of Life

But that everyone may find particular reasons for humiliating himself, I shall now propose such as may be suitable to the state of each. To commence with bishops: I say that a bishop has great matter for humility before God, seeing how little care he takes of his people despite the example of our Savior, who did not hesitate to give His life for the souls whom His Father had confided to Him. Alas! How can anyone render an account of each individual under his charge if he does not even know his flock by sight?

What shall I say of the priest? What should be his humility when he hears these words of Jesus Christ, "So likewise every one of you that doth not renounce all that he possesseth, cannot be my disciple" (Luke 14:33), and when he compares the recklessness of his behavior with the sanctity of the Victim whom he holds in his hands, and of whom he is the sacrificer?

What ought also be the humility of the preacher when he reflects that he is called to the ministry of the Redeemer of the world and that his life is so different from that of his Master? Let him consider the life that Jesus Christ led in the desert before He preached the gospel, and let him form himself on this model. Unhappy is he who does not take care to make his conduct conformable to the doctrine that he teaches. Let him remember that the word of God is a holy word, and that an impure mouth is unworthy to announce it. Let him fear this terrible reproach that God made to the preachers by His prophet: "But to the sinner God hath said: Why dost thou declare my justices, and take my covenant in thy mouth? Seeing thou hast hated discipline: and hast cast my words behind thee" (Ps. 49:16–17). If the great Apostle feared to be a reprobate and a castaway when teaching others the way of salvation, should not the preacher tremble and keep himself in humility?

Since St. Paul assures us that "knowledge puffeth up" (1 Cor. 8:1), those who instruct others should humble themselves; for when anyone persuades himself that he knows enough, he knows too much, and the same saint warns us not to have more wisdom than it behooves us to have.

Those who submit themselves to the guidance of a master to be instructed in the sciences will not want matter for humility: for besides their want of knowledge, they should count for nothing all they learn if they have any other end in their studies than the glory of God and the salvation of their neighbor.

Religious also have much reason to humble themselves before God when they compare themselves to infidels, Jews, and to Christians living in the world; considering that, although they have been gifted with the light of faith and called to the happy state of the religious life by a singular favor, they are perhaps enemies of God, even when esteemed His most faithful servants; and that, though living in the house of God as His children, they are very far from the sanctity of their heavenly Father. Alas! If the house of God is a house of prayer, what humility ought not those to have who live there without devotion? If the royal prophet considered himself happier in being despised than in living in splendor among sinners, what can be said of Religious who remain in God's house with constraint or, at least, are not grateful for the happiness that they enjoy?

There are two kinds of Religious: some have liberty to go into diverse places and to converse with men; others live in solitude and remain shut up in their monasteries. The former should not be puffed up because their life is more conformable to that of the apostles; on the contrary, they should persuade themselves that the journeys and labors in which their state engages them are the means that God has given them to do penance for their sins. Neither should solitary recluses esteem themselves more perfect than others; rather ought they to believe that God has separated them from intercourse with men because He knew their weakness, and that they would have been undoubtedly lost in any other state of life.

Even kings and princes, however elevated they may be above other men, have a subject for humility in their own grandeur, since Jesus Christ always avoided it and hid Himself when they wished to make Him king. How can they accept, with so much ease, a burden that our Savior was not willing to take upon Himself?

Is it not a great matter for humility for a courtier to consider how many dangers he exposes himself to, how many annoyances and fatigues he suffers to merit the favor of his prince, and what little pains he takes to make himself agreeable to God, his sovereign Lord? Alas! If he brought to God's service the least part of that diligence with which he devotes himself entirely to the service of a mortal king, he would soon become king himself, since "to serve God is to reign."

A soldier should remember that it is for the defense of religion and the gospel that he carries his sword and not to satisfy his revengeful passion that makes him a persecutor of Jesus Christ and the gospel, of which he ought to be the defender. Let him humble himself, then, for being so fastidious about what regards his own honor and for having so little zeal to sustain the honor of God.

A judge who is anxious his sentence should be executed in all its rigor should reflect on the rigorous justice of God and consider what Holy Scripture teaches, that the judges of the world shall be judged with an extreme severity.

Christian ladies should consider how contrary to the spirit of Jesus Christ are the luxuries and vanities that surround them; and that the costly apparel, the necklaces and bracelets with which they adorn themselves, correspond but poorly with the robe of infamy with which our Savior was clothed in the house of Herod, and to the chains with which He was loaded for their love.

But because it would be endless to enumerate here all the different states of life, it suffices to say that there is not one that cannot furnish abundant matter for humility, provided we take the trouble of thinking seriously.

What Our Own Faculties and Senses Teach Us About Humility

Thus, what remains for us now is to humble ourselves at the sight of the things that are within us, such as the faculties of the body and the soul. To commence with the memory, is it not strange that a faculty that has been given to us by God to make us remember Him has been filled only with the things of the earth? God has made use of various and diverse means to prevent our falling into forgetfulness of eternal things. He has ordered us to take ashes at the commencement of Lent to make us recollect what we are. He exhorts us unceasingly in the Bible to remember how great is our weakness and how manifold are His bounties: "In all thy works remember thy last end, and thou shalt never sin" (Sir. 7:40); "Remember my poverty, and transgression, the wormwood, and the gall" (Lam. 3:19).

What blindness, then, to employ our memory only with useless, and sometimes even criminal, things, to detach it from what can alone contribute to our perfection, and to deprive ourselves of the consolation there is in the remembrance of God. "My soul is troubled exceedingly," said the prophet (Ps. 6:4); but "I remembered God, and was delighted" (Ps. 76:4).

Nor have we made a better use of our understanding than of our memory. The perishable things of earth have been its ordinary occupation. Our intellect was bestowed on us by God to be devoted to the contemplation of the Sovereign Good, and we have turned it from the sight of its true object to apply it to trifles. But what shall I say of the will, which, having been given to us by God to love Him above all things, is so readily abandoned to the love of what is most base, the very thought of which ought to humble us? How frail is this will, how easily drawn from God to please the senses! It could merit in Heaven a glory equal to that of the seraphim by loving its Creator, and it has become instead like the instinct of beasts, and worthy of Hell, by the baseness of the things on which it fixes its affections.

Remember, then, Christian soul, that the misuse of your faculties is a great subject of humility for you. Therefore, often reflect on this, and do not allow so salutary a thought to stray from your mind. Reproach yourself for having effaced the image of God; ask your memory why it had forgotten Him; your understanding why it had become so blind; and your will why it had permitted itself to be led captive. Having forsaken God, who is their true nourishment, the faculties of your soul have wandered in search of poisonous herbs, capable only of producing their death.

And in order that there be nothing in you that may not minister to humility, study what use you have made of your senses. Consider that God has given you eyes to recognize His perfections in those of creatures, to love and glorify Him above all things, and that you have made use of these eyes for your own gratification and to usurp over His creatures a dominion that belongs only to the Creator.

Again, ponder that you have closed your ears to the divine inspirations and have opened them to the hissings of the serpent. That your tongue, instead of blessing God, is occupied in slandering your neighbor. That you have been so careful in avoiding all kinds of foul stench and so negligent in avoiding sin. That the maxims of Jesus Christ have appeared so hard and troublesome to you, and that those of the world have delighted you.

Weep, then, Christian soul, for the misuse of your senses, in considering the end for which God has given them to you and how you have misapplied them. And if this is not all enough to overwhelm you with sorrow and shame, remember that your head is without thorns yet our Savior's was crowned with them for your love; that His feet and hands were pierced with nails to merit for you the liberty of the children of God; that you have used your feet to persecute Him, and your hands to inflict new wounds upon Him by your criminal actions.

In a word, if you wish not to flatter yourself, you will find nothing within you that will not be a cause for humility; no, not even your good works, since, by considering the inclination you have to evil and the difficulty you feel in doing good, you will be surprised that a sinner like yourself can do anything agreeable to God. For a good action is the fruit of the grace of Jesus Christ and not of nature or of sin; and the little good you do comes not from yourself but from God, who begins and finishes it in you.

Part III

Considering Heavenly Things

Since no words can express the sentiments of humility we ought to have at the sight of the things that are on this earth, how shall we dare to raise our eyes toward Heaven? The consideration alone of the stars, whose movements are so equal and so regular, should remind us of our own inconstancy and waywardness. They receive and communicate their influence according to the order that their Creator has prescribed for them; man alone deviates from this by refusing to share with his neighbor the favors that he has received from God, and to accept those that God still offers him.

The sky and the planets illumine themselves with the light of the sun, and man refuses to clothe himself with the light of the Sun of Justice, and prefers darkness to light.

Let us humble ourselves in considering the purity of the angels and how seldom we have hearkened to their most prudent, salutary, and charitable inspirations. Let us compare the ardor of the Seraphim with our weakness and tepidity, the light and knowledge of the Cherubim with our blindness and ignorance.

But, as some may contend that man, being but dust and ashes, should not compare himself with these blessed spirits, who are so perfect, I shall speak more of the saints, who have been men like ourselves, and the weakness of whose flesh did not prevent them from undertaking great things for the glory of God. Alas! What humility for us to compare our daintiness with the torments of the martyrs, our negligence with the zeal of the confessors, our impurity with the purity of the virgins and, above all, with that of the Queen of Virgins.

Contemplating the Holy Trinity

It must be acknowledged, however, that what ought to confound us most of all is the consideration that the sufferings of our Savior are the effects of our crimes; that our sloth has nailed His feet to the Cross; that our disobedience has opened His side; that our criminal actions have pierced

His hands; that our uncharitable speech has made Him taste the bitterness of vinegar and gall; that our pride has crowned Him with thorns; indeed, that there is nothing in Jesus Christ that ought not to fill us with shame, since His torments and humiliations are the work of our hands.

But what ought to be the sentiments of a sinner at the sight of the Holy Trinity, after having found a subject of humility even in the devils? How shall he dare to regard the Eternal Father? That Father of Mercy sent His only Son into this world to draw us from the power of darkness, and instead of recognizing Him as our legitimate Sovereign, we have crucified Him? What shall we answer when He demands an account of all the talents of nature and grace that He has bestowed on us?

What shall we reply to the Son when He requires an account of His Blood and His death; when He reproaches us with our ingratitude and says to us: "I have descended from Heaven, I have left the bosom of My Father and My own Kingdom for your salvation, ungrateful and insensible sinner; and you have not wished to forsake your sins to testify your gratitude. I have loved you first; I protected you before you had done anything in My service. O, hard and flinty heart, you see Me bound to a pillar, all covered with the wounds I have received for your love, and you still wish to remain attached to your crimes. O, unheard of ingratitude! The beasts serve Me, the herbs and plants praise Me; man alone refuses to recognize Me and revolts against his Lord. I have become for you a Lamb full of mildness and sweetness, and you have always been a furious and intractable lion. You have crowned Me with thorns by your pride, and I have crowned you with glory by My humility; you have loaded Me with chains, and I have delivered you from the slavery of the devil. I have sought you in your wanderings, I have invited, I have begged you to return to Me; I have forgotten nothing to make you love Me, and you have not ceased to persecute Me and to renew the dolors of My Passion by the multitude of your sins.

"Humble yourself, then, ungrateful soul, and recollect that in the terrible day of My judgment, you shall be filled with an inconceivable humility if you do not prevent it, in this life, by a sincere repentance of your sins. Consider how I have sought you, I who am your God; that I have feared to lose you, I who had no need of you; that I have redeemed you at the price of My Blood and My life, and that you have fled from Me as if I were your enemy, without fearing either My hatred or the rigor of My judgment.

"Reflect on the unhappy state to which you are reduced by so fatal a blindness. It is time to recognize your wanderings and do penance for them, since you know neither the day nor the hour of your death."

What will you reply to the Holy Spirit, to whom you have so often refused an entrance into your heart, and whom you have driven away to put the devil in His place? "Be ashamed of yourselves, O foolish and insensible men! You were created to be the children of your Father who is in Heaven, and you have acted ever in a manner unworthy of the nobility of your origin. The mildness of your Heavenly Father is infinite. He is still ready to pardon you; and you, by the greatest of all injustices, not only refuse to pardon those who have offended you, but you even offend Him from whom you receive unceasing benefits. His goodness is unbounded, since He preserves His enemies and does good to those who despise Him; and you, by an intolerable hardness, do evil to Him who loves you. Finally, the wisdom and providence with which He governs the universe are admirable; and it appears that you have resolved to disturb the harmony of it, and to ruin all things, in order to reign in the world with the more assurance. 'Shall you alone,' said God, by the prophet Isaiah, 'dwell in the midst of the earth?' " (Isa. 5:8).

Concluding Thoughts

This matter is of unlimited application; but what I have said is sufficient to make those who wish to acquire perfect humility understand the advantage they can draw from this exercise, provided they apply themselves to it seriously. And certainly, each one ought to devote himself to it with the more care, as there is no more efficacious means for making great progress in virtue in a short time than the knowledge of one's own weakness. This is a most solid foundation upon which we can raise a sure edifice of Christian perfection—and without which we are in continual danger of falling. The greatest graces, without humility, are the most dangerous snares; and the spiritual consolations that we receive in prayer, and that are so useful to detach our souls from earth and to lead them to a high degree of sanctity, change for the proud into so many illusions, which the devil makes use of for their destruction.

Therefore, if we wish to walk safely in the way of perfection, we should commence by knowing and humbling ourselves, for God never abandons those who take care to preserve themselves in humility, according to the words of the prophet: "A contrite and humbled heart, O God, thou wilt not despise" (Ps. 50:19). Humility is that wedding garment without which no one is admitted to the

Divine Espousals, and with which Jesus Christ was the first to invest Himself: "All the day long my shame is before me," said He, by the same prophet, "and the confusion of my face hath covered me" (Ps. 43:16). If the adorable face that makes the joy of angels and of saints was covered with humility, what ought to be the sentiments of a sinner, and how shall he dare to appear before his God without being penetrated with this salutary humility, since it is written: "Let them that detract me be clothed with shame: and let them be covered with confusion as with a double cloak" (Ps. 108:29)? Neither should the just man be dispensed from self-humiliation if he wishes to preserve his innocence: "My hand made all these things, and all these things were made," says the Lord, "But to whom shall I have respect, but to him that is poor and little, and of a contrite spirit, and that trembleth at my words?" (Isa. 66:2). It appears that the saints feel humble even in Heaven, at seeing how much the greatness of their recompense surpasses the merit of their actions; and they say to God with astonishment, "Lord, when is it that You have seen us hungry, and have not given us to eat?" That is to say, "Lord, what have we done to merit the glory you have prepared for us?" If it is, then, true that humility raises us to the possession of God, is it not reasonable that we should embrace the practice of it with the same ardor as a drowning man clings to a plank in shipwreck, in order to save ourselves from the perils to which this miserable life unceasingly exposes us, and to arrive at length, by the mercy of God, at the port of eternal life? Amen.

Reflections on Christian Action: Exercises for Acting in the Spirit of Jesus Christ

Dedication

From St. Francis Borgia to His Aunt,
the Abbess of St. Clare of Gandia

Madam,

For a long time, I have desired to make you a present that would be agreeable to you, in the hope of atoning for all the grief that I have caused you by my sins and the irregularities of my life.

Seeing, however, that I could not acquit myself of this obligation, except by good works, and, moreover, well knowing myself incapable of performing any other good work, I felt that I ought to try to unite myself to Jesus Christ by meditating upon His holy actions in order that their merit might give some value to mine and render this gift more worthy of being offered to you. It is with this view that I have undertaken the present little work, in which I have collected together several pious practices, that I might present them to you in expiation for my past faults. I offer them to you, then, and I most humbly implore of you to assist me with the help of your prayers, in order that I may myself practice what I teach to others. I hope you will not refuse me this request, had you no other reason for granting it than the example of our Lord Jesus Christ, who not only has helped us to satisfy the divine Justice but has been pleased Himself to become a victim of propitiation for our sins.

Since the Holy Scriptures teach us that God will reward us according to our works, we ought to follow the advice of the Apostle, who exhorts us to do good while there is yet time because the night is coming during which no one can work. Thus, when the thought of doing a good action presents itself to our mind, if reason approves and the will agrees—because this action is conformable to the rules of Holy Scripture and may contribute to the glory of God and the salvation of our neighbor—we should be extremely diligent in executing it, because it is certain that a man loses much when he neglects to perform the good that he can do, and that it would have been incomparably better not to have had the thought than to have failed in accomplishing it after having had it. It is for this reason that Hell is said to be full of good intentions; for though it is true that good intentions are useless without good works, it is also true that no more efficacious means exists of obtaining eternal salvation than the performance of good works, in whatever state a man may be. If he is in sin, these aid him to repent; and if he is in grace, they help him to obtain from God the gift of perseverance, according to the words of Scripture: "He that hearkeneth to me, shall not be confounded: and they that work by me, shall not sin" (Sir. 24:30). Let us imitate, then, the prophet Isaiah, who said that his works were in God, and apply ourselves to do all our actions in God and for God, since there is no other way of rendering them agreeable and meritorious for eternal life. Let us endeavor to unite all our actions to those which Jesus Christ our Savior was pleased to perform for our salvation while He lived on earth, by the great charity that He had for us, so that they may thus become salutary and well-pleasing to God through the merits of Christ. It was for this purpose He became man: He embraced our poverty only to communicate to us His riches. For this reason, He has been pleased to eat, to fast, to sleep, to watch; He subjected Himself to the various duties of man's life in order that they might be sources of benediction to us and that each one might profit by them according to the measure of God's grace, by offering them through Himself to the Eternal Father. But to render this exercise easier, I shall here propose several practices that each one can make use of, conformably to his lights and his devotion.

Part I

The Spirit of Jesus in the Particular Actions of the Day

You ought, O devout soul, to make yourself as familiar as you possibly can with these exercises in order that your actions, which are sterile and imperfect in themselves, may become holy and salutary, and that they may merit to be presented to God as an agreeable sacrifice. You should commence by the ordinary actions of each day, which are common to all; and I can assure you that if you are faithful to this practice, besides acquiring, by degrees, a great facility for acting holily in all the other circumstances of life, you will find in it wondrous sweetness and consolation.

Now this practice consists in having three motives in each action that you perform: first, to humble yourself before God; second, to thank Him for His graces; and third, to ask Him for those of which you have need.

While Dressing in the Morning

1. Enter into a profound sentiment of humility in considering that you are well clothed and that Jesus Christ was fastened naked to a Cross for love of you.
2. Thank Him for having assumed our nature, although He knew at the time how ungrateful we should be for this favor; and also for having given us clothes to cover us, although we have so often despised the nuptial robe of grace with which He clothed us.
3. While dressing yourself, you are performing one of the works of mercy, which is to clothe the naked: implore Him to accept this action in consideration of the garment of ignominy with which He was covered in the palace of Herod.

On Entering a Church

1. Humble yourself in considering how unworthy your imperfections render you to enter the house of God, where He is adored by angels with so much awe and purity.

2. Thank Him that, after having so often strayed far from Him, owing to the enormity of your sins, He is well pleased to receive you into His house; that He even seeks for you and begs you to enter.
3. Ask Him for the grace to offer yourself to Him with the same love with which the Blessed Virgin presented her Son in the Temple; with the desire of becoming yourself a temple of God, in which the Holy Spirit may dwell.

When Beginning to Pray

1. Humble yourself before God, repeating the words of the publican, "O God, be merciful to me a sinner" (Luke 18:13), and reflect on the multitude of your sins.
2. Return thanks to Jesus Christ for having vouchsafed to pray for you, in order that your petitions may be granted by the merit of His prayer.
3. Beseech Him, by the merit of the prayer that He offered up for all sinners in the desert, to grant you the graces that He has Himself ordered you to ask from Him in the Lord's Prayer, which you should recite once with great attention and devotion.

On Assisting at Mass

1. Reflect humbly with how little devotion you come to see and adore your God. Reproach yourself that the continuation of so great a benefit is the cause of the light esteem in which you hold it, instead of the cause, as it ought to be, of an increase in your respect and love; since God renders His favors so common only to make better known the great charity that He has for you.
2. Thank Him for making you resemble the angels each time you adore Him with true faith: for these blessed spirits are always employed in His presence, praising and glorifying Him unceasingly.
3. Since this sacrifice is offered to God in memory of the sacrifice of Calvary, ask of Him, through the merits of His precious Blood, the grace to cleanse yourself in it from all your sins and to efface them by the abundance of your tears, that the old man may die within you and the new man live therein.

During Lunch

1. Humble yourself for having betrayed Him who gives you food and for being so ungrateful for the benefits that you have received.
2. Thank Him for having so long preserved you and for having nourished you with so much care, even when you were His enemy.
3. Beg Him, by the charity with which He fed so great a multitude in the desert, to give you the celestial nourishment of His grace, and that this may be your daily bread.

When Performing Some Act of Charity

1. Humble yourself that having so often contributed to the disedification of your neighbor by your bad example, God is yet pleased to make use of you in an affair so important as that of the salvation of others. To effect that salvation, He sent His beloved Son into this world.
2. Thank Him that, being in want of nothing, He nevertheless accepts the little good that you do for Him, as though you were necessary to Him.

3. Implore Him by that charity with which He said that His business was to employ Himself in the service and glory of His Father, that He will give you the grace to occupy yourself only in holy actions, in order that they may serve for the advancement of His glory.

At Evening Prayer

1. Consider that you speak to a God before whom the angels tremble with awe and fear.
2. Thank Him for having given you the courage to pray to Him by a commandment full of goodness and mercy.
3. Entreat Him, by that same resignation that caused Him to sweat drops of Blood in the Garden of Olives and made Him say, "My Father … not as I will, but as thou wilt" (Matt. 26:39), to give you the grace to be always perfectly united to His holy will, in life and in death.

At Supper

1. Reflect on the sins that you have committed during the day and eat your food with sorrow, according to the words of the prophet: "For I did eat ashes like bread, and mingled my drink with weeping" (Ps. 101:10).

2. Return thanks to God for the goodness with which He has repeated in the evening a favor for which you had so badly thanked Him in the morning.
3. Ask Him, by the love that caused Him to give Himself for your nourishment in the Last Supper, to prepare your heart to receive Him with humility and to live so united to Him by charity that He may be always in you and you in Him.

Before Retiring to Rest

1. Picture to yourself Jesus Christ nailed to the Cross, praying for you with so much love, while you are without love for Him and show no grief for the pains that He endures for love of you.
2. Thank Him for having been pleased to die to give you life.
3. Beseech Him, by the great sufferings He endured in His last moments, and by the grief that His Blessed Mother felt on seeing Him expire, to grant you the grace to think of His most holy death when your last hour shall come, that it may become precious before God by the merit of His own death.

When Undressing

1. Consider that you undress yourself in order to sleep with more comfort, while Jesus Christ was born on straw for love of you and had no place to rest His head.
2. Thank Him for having suffered so many hardships to merit for you the grace to renounce the devil.
3. Pray that, by the extreme torment He endured when, before crucifying Him, they tore off the garment that adhered to His sacred wounds, He will deliver you from your vicious habits, so that, being entirely divested of all affection to earthly things, you may embrace the Cross, may die upon it with Jesus Christ, and may merit afterward that robe of glory that God has prepared for those who love Him.

Part II

The Spirit of Jesus in All Our Acts

It would render this exercise too long were I to apply this practice to all our actions in detail, as they are almost without number. But I have here marked those that are common to everyone.

On Our Exterior Actions

Those who, with the desire of greater perfection, would wish to extend this practice of emulating Jesus to other actions can make use of the following:

- *When standing*: Represent to yourself our Savior and reflect on the manner in which He stood before His judges.

- *When sitting*: Remember how, when Jesus Christ was seated, the Jews made Him suffer a thousand outrages, saying to Him in mockery, "Hail, King of the Jews!"
- *When walking*: Think of Jesus Christ going to Samaria and Calvary.
- *When you are fatigued*: Recollect how our Savior, being fatigued on the road, seated Himself on a stone to rest.
- *When riding*: Figure to yourself our Lord entering Jerusalem on an ass.
- *When visiting the sick*: Think how Jesus Christ not only visited them with much charity but also cured them.
- *When your good works are censured*: Remember how those of our Lord were blamed, all holy as they were, and how they murmured at His curing the sick on the Sabbath day.
- *When you are answered with contempt and treated with disrespect*: Think of the indignity with which our Savior was treated in the house of Caiphas when a soldier said insolently to Him, "Is it thus Thou answerest the High Priest?" and even dared to strike that sacred face, which is the mirror of angels and the consolation of saints.

- *When you are hungry*: Consider the hunger that Jesus suffered during the forty days He fasted in the desert.
- *When you are cold*: Reflect on the cold that our Infant Savior endured in the manger at Bethlehem, when He willed to be born in the severest season of the year, without fire and without other bed than the straw on which He was laid.
- *When you are thirsty*: Think of the vinegar and gall with which He was presented on the Cross, when He said, "I thirst."
- *When you are disturbed from your sleep*: Recollect how they awoke Jesus Christ when He slept in the boat.
- *When your friends abandon you in want*: Consider how our Lord was forsaken by His disciples at the time of His Passion.
- *When you are obliged to leave persons whom you love*: Think of the separation of Jesus Christ from His holy Mother.
- *If it happens that you are insulted in public*: Reflect in what state Pilate showed Jesus Christ to the people, saying, "Behold the Man."
- *If you are accused of any fault of which you are innocent*: Represent to yourself the falsehoods and calumnies with which they charged Him in the house of Caiphas.

- *If you are condemned without reason*: Remember the unjust sentence that was pronounced against Jesus Christ.
- *When you are ill and endure great pain*: Figure to yourself the scourging, the crowning with thorns, and the Crucifixion. Jesus was covered with wounds from the top of His head to the sole of His foot; He wished that no part of His Body should be exempt from pain in order that we might suffer nothing that He had not endured before us, and that we might be obliged to offer all our sufferings to Him.
- *Finally, when you are at the hour of your death*: Abandon your spirit with lively faith into His hands and remember the words He said to His Father when dying: "Father, into thy hands I commend my spirit" (Luke 23:46). Thus, by making Him a sacrifice of your life in consideration of His death, you will merit to live eternally with Him in glory. Amen.

This exercise will be of marvelous utility to those who will practice it with faithfulness and love. But as most of the things of which we have spoken up to the present regard only our exterior actions, I have thought that it would be still better to apply this practice to our interior actions and that the advantages that may be drawn from it would be far greater, since those who give themselves to spiritual things feel the necessities of the body much less than those of the soul. Thus, so that everyone may find in this exercise what will satisfy his devotion, I have added the following considerations.

On Our Interior Actions, Thoughts, and Feelings

- *When your neighbor regrets the counsel that you had charitably given him*: Offer this refusal to our Lord in remembrance of how little profit men have drawn from His holy doctrine.
- *When you see your brother offend* God, *and when you feel grieved at it*: Offer your grief to Jesus Christ and reflect on the displeasure that He showed when He publicly drove from the Temple the money changers who profaned it.
- *If any of your friends stray from the path of virtue*: Think of the misfortune of Judas, who abandoned the source of all good, and try to feel the same feeling at the fall of your friend as Jesus felt at that of His apostle.
- *When it happens that you reflect on the small number of zealous pastors there are in the Church*: Remember how

our Lord complained when He said these words: "The harvest indeed is great, but the labourers are few" (Luke 10:2).

- *When God gives you grace to weep for your sins*: Join your grief to the grief that your sins caused Jesus Christ, who knew them long before you had committed them. Unite them to that which He Himself suffered to efface them. Bless Him and return Him a thousand thanks for having been willing to afflict Himself for your offenses.
- *When you see anyone fall who is already advanced in the way of perfection*: Think of the sorrow our Lord felt at the fall of St. Peter, who had already recognized Him as the Son of the Living God and who had seen Him transfigured on Mount Tabor.
- *When you are attacked with the temptations of the devil*: Remember those temptations with which Jesus Christ was assailed in the desert.
- *When you are afflicted at seeing that the wicked cannot endure the company of the good*: Consider how our Savior was persecuted by a people whom He had laden with benefits and to whom He had given the sincerest proofs of His love and of His charity.

- *When you reflect on the crimes of a town or of an entire nation*: Join the sorrow you feel for them to the tears that our Lord shed over the destruction of Jerusalem.
- *When you know that any one has fallen into infidelity or doubt*: Feel afflicted at this, and think at the same time of the displeasure that Jesus Christ felt at seeing that His disciples, by their want of faith, had lost the power of casting out devils, which made Him say these words: "O incredulous generation, how long shall I be with you? how long shall I suffer you?" (Mark 9:18).
- *When the wicked insult the good*: Remember the insults that our Redeemer endured on the Cross when they said to Him in mockery, "He saved others, himself he cannot save" (Matt. 27:42).
- *When you see someone die who has led a wicked life*: Think with sorrow on what our Lord felt when considering how few persons would accept the grace and salvation offered to all by His death.
- *When your prayer is accompanied by aridity and desolation*: Call to mind what Jesus Christ suffered when He said to His Father, "My God, my God, why hast thou forsaken me?" (Matt. 27:46).

- *When you hear anyone blaspheme the name of God*: Imagine the affliction our Lord felt at knowing that His name, all holy as it is, would be blasphemed by men.
- *When your soul feels separated from God and sighs to be reunited to Him by charity and to be delivered from the dangers of this state*: Consider what the Heart of Jesus suffered when, in His infinite charity, He asked His Eternal Father that we might be united to Him, in these wonderful words: "That they all may be one, as thou, Father, in me, and I in thee; that they also may be one in us" (John 17:21).

Concluding Thoughts

Who, then, is so negligent and so little desirous for his own good as to refuse the precious manna and inestimable treasures of grace that are offered to him? Who will be ungrateful enough toward Jesus Christ not to testify his love for Him by the practice of at least a part of these exercises we have proposed—exercises that are so excellent, so full of love, and so necessary to salvation?

O, devout soul, deprive not yourself of so great a blessing: consider that what your God asks of you is little in comparison to what He Himself promises you in return.

He asks from you those things only that you are obliged to do every day and that are common to everybody; and He asks them from you only that they may not be lost to yourself. In a word, you must walk, you must eat, you must work, you must sometimes fall ill, and, finally, you must die. And furthermore, it is certain that if you do all these things only for your own satisfaction, or to please the world, they will be all the more difficult, inasmuch as you will not find the solid consolation you would have had if you had held this view, and there will remain for you nothing but grief and remorse for having labored without result. Consider, therefore, seriously: if you wish in the future to suffer the crosses you meet with for the love of Jesus Christ, you will find consolation in your troubles, because our Lord is always in the company of the afflicted; and you will finally receive a recompense that "eye hath not seen, nor ear heard, neither hath it entered into the heart of man" (1 Cor. 2:9).

Oh! How unspeakable is the happiness that God has prepared for those who serve Him; and how much ought we not to regret the many opportunities we have lost of meriting it; and how earnestly should we avail ourselves of every opportunity that will in future present itself! For it is certain that if we apply our senses and the powers of our soul in following the path that Jesus Christ has marked out for us, all our actions will be holy, and our conscience will remind us of what our Lord said in the Gospel: "He that followeth me, walketh not in darkness" (John 8:12), because Jesus is "the true light, which enlighteneth every man that cometh into this world" (John 1:9); and He has been the pilot of all those who have arrived at the port of eternal life, which I pray we may also reach by His grace, there to bless the Father, the Son, and the Holy Spirit, forever and ever. Amen.

Reflections for Holy Communion

Those to whom God has given the grace to approach frequently the holy Eucharist should devote the three days that precede it to preparing themselves for this holy action and the three days that follow it to returning thanks to God for so inestimable a favor.

Part I

Preparation for Holy Communion

First Day

We should beg the Eternal Father—by that ineffable charity with which He loved the world, even to giving His only Son for it; by the merits and tears of the prophets and patriarchs; and by those ardent desires with which He inflamed their hearts to make them ask with so much earnestness and prayer the coming of His Son, whom they recognized by a divine light as their only Redeemer—we should, I say, implore this heavenly Father to prepare our hearts, since our Savior Himself assures us that no one can go to Him but by His Father: "No man," said He, "can come to me, except the Father, who hath sent me, draw him; and I will raise him up in the last day" (John 6:44).

Therefore, to obtain this grace, let us recite in the morning the following prayer of the Church:

> O Lord, inflame our hearts, and prepare them to receive Thine only Son, that, our souls being purified by His coming, we may worthily worship Thy sovereign Majesty. This we implore through Jesus Christ Thy Son, who, being God, liveth and reigneth with Thee, in the unity of the Holy Spirit, forever and ever. Amen.

In order that this desire may not quit us during the day, on account of the cares and embarrassments of temporal things, we should excite ourselves from time to time by these devout aspirations: "Send forth, O Lord, the lamb, the ruler of the earth, from Petra of the desert, to the mount of the daughter of Sion" (Isa. 16:1). Or the following: "And who shall be able to think of the day of his coming? And who shall stand to see him? For he is like a refining fire, and like the fuller's herb" (Mal. 3:2).

Ask, therefore, for an increase of your good desires and for that purity of heart that will make you worthy of receiving this spotless Lamb.

In the evening, address yourself to the Blessed Virgin and beg her to obtain for you the grace to prepare well for receiving her Son. After this, recite nine Hail Marys:

- The first in memory of the desire with which this Mother of sinners awaited the coming of their Redeemer, and to obtain, by her intercession and merits, an ardent desire of the glory of God and the salvation of our neighbor.
- The second to honor the disposition she always had for divine grace and to ask her for a holy preparation for Communion.
- The third in memory of the humility with which she received Jesus Christ at the moment of the Incarnation, and to obtain the grace of receiving Him in the Holy Eucharist with a profound humility.
- The fourth in memory of the love with which she embraced Him, after having brought Him into the world, in the stable at Bethlehem; and that she may obtain for us also the grace of embracing Him with an ardent love in Holy Communion.
- The fifth to commemorate the grief with which she received her Son into her arms when He was taken

down from the Cross, and to obtain the grace to receive Him with a tender sympathy for His Passion.

- The sixth in memory of the faith and confidence with which she awaited the Resurrection of our Savior, and to merit the grace of receiving Him with an increase of faith and confidence.
- The seventh in honor of the preparation she made for the reception of the Holy Spirit, and to have a larger abundance of graces in order to approach the holy Eucharist with greater purity and perfection.
- The eighth to beseech her, by the fervor with which she received Jesus Christ in the most holy Sacrament of the altar, to obtain for us the grace to receive Him with a devotion worthy of this mystery of charity.
- The ninth to supplicate her, by the joy with which her well-beloved Son received her into Heaven on the day of her Assumption, to merit for us the grace of receiving Him into our hearts with a plenitude of spiritual joy and gladness.

Second Day

We should beg Jesus Christ, by the great charity that induced Him to become man to deliver us from death, to give us life by His coming into our hearts, since He assures us that if we do not eat His flesh, we shall not have life in us.

In the morning, pray:

> O Jesus, make known Thy power, and come down from Heaven to this earth to deliver us by Thy protection from the perils into which our sins are leading us, and to cure us of all our weakness by the strength of Thy grace; Thou, who being God, lives and reigns with God the Father, in the unity of the Holy Spirit, forever and ever. Amen.

We should devote this day to purifying our conscience in the Blood of Jesus Christ. Therefore, it will be advisable to meditate on the seven occasions on which He shed His precious Blood[3] and to see what virtues and perfections we fail in, so that when we receive Him into our hearts, we may ask Him to relieve our poverty by the abundance of His celestial riches. For it is from Him that we must expect all the graces that are necessary for a holy preparation.

[3] These are: Jesus' circumcision, His suffering in the Garden of Gethsemane, the scourging at the pillar, the crown of thorns, the carrying of His Cross, His Crucifixion, and the piercing of His side.

During the day, we should frequently make use of the following words to rouse our languid heart: "O, King of Peoples and Desired of Nations, come to save the creature whom Thou has formed out of dust."

In the evening, let us have recourse to the Mother of God, from whose hands we have received this Celestial Bread. Let us beg her, by the extreme dolors she felt at the foot of the Cross, to obtain for us from God the grace to participate in the Passion and death of her adorable Son. Let us then recite five Our Fathers and five Hail Marys to ask that the five wounds of Jesus Christ may be eternally engraved in our hearts.

Third Day

We should beg the Holy Spirit—by the charity with which He filled the apostles when He descended upon them in the form of tongues of fire, and by the preparation they made to receive so precious a gift—that He may Himself prepare our hearts to receive Him and inflame them with the fire of His love, so that all our senses and faculties may be occupied in loving Him who has given Himself to us through love.

In the morning, pray:

We implore Thee, O Lord, that the Holy Spirit, who proceeds from Thee, may enlighten our minds and teach us all truths, according to the promise of Thy Son, who, being God, lives and reigns with Thee, in the unity of the Holy Spirit, forever and ever. Amen.

We should, on this day, renew all our good desires and endeavor to make them the more fervent, as Jesus Christ is the more near to us. And as it is usual to shut the doors of a house when it is being adorned within, so we should close our senses and faculties to all exterior things and often testify by the following words the holy impatience we have of being united to our Sovereign Good: "Come, O Holy Spirit, visit the souls of Thy servants, and fill with Thy grace the hearts Thou has created." Or "Arise, be enlightened, O Jerusalem: for thy light is come, and the glory of the Lord is risen upon thee" (Isa. 60:1).

In the evening, we should entreat the spouse of the Holy Spirit, by the grace with which He filled her when she became the temple of the most Holy Trinity, to inflame our hearts with the love of her Son, so that we may be worthy to receive Him within us according to the promise He made us in the Holy Gospel: "If any one love me, he will keep my word, and my Father will love him, and we will come to him, and will make our abode with him" (John 14:23). We should then recite seven Hail Marys to obtain the seven gifts of the Holy Spirit through the intercession of His most holy spouse.

Part II

Thanksgiving after Communion

We should spend the three days after Communion in returning thanks to Jesus Christ for so inestimable a favor.

First Day

We should thank the Eternal Father for the benefit of creation, which He renews so often in the Blessed Eucharist. By an act of wondrous goodness, He created us like unto Himself and imprinted on us His own image; but as we had nearly effaced all traces of this, He wished to re-establish in us this divine image by the Communion of the Body of Jesus Christ. It is only right, then, to testify the most ardent gratitude for such unspeakable goodness, and to invite on this day all the creatures of Heaven to thank Him for us after the following manner:

> O all you works of the Lord, bless the Lord; praise and exalt Him above all forever.
>
> O all you angels of the Lord, bless the Lord; bless the Lord, you heavens.
>
> O all you waters that are above the heavens, bless the Lord; bless the Lord, all you powers of the Lord.
>
> O you sun and moon, bless the Lord; bless the Lord, you stars of Heaven.
>
> O you fire and heat, bless the Lord; bless the Lord, you winter and summer,
>
> O you dews and hoar frost, bless the Lord; bless the Lord, you frost and cold.
>
> O you ice and snow, bless the Lord; bless the Lord, you nights and days.
>
> O you light and darkness, bless the Lord; bless the Lord, you lightnings and clouds.[4]

[4] Adapted from the traditional *Canticum Trium Puerorum* (Canticle of the Three Youths), the song of Shadrach, Meshach, and Abednego as they stood in the furnace

Let us thus excite the works of the Lord to return Him thanks for us in whom He has worked effects like those that all these creatures produced by giving us the Body of His only begotten Son. He has raised us to the condition of the angels, and, earthly as we are, He has made us all heavenly. He has purified us by the saving waters of His grace and by the abundance of our tears; He has enlightened us with the rays of the Sun of Justice; He has melted the ice of our hearts, and He has warmed our coldness by the fire of His divine love; indeed, He has dissipated all our darkness by the splendor of His light.

We should in this manner apply verses of the canticles to the particular graces each one of us has received from God.

We should animate ourselves during the day with great sentiments of gratitude, and we should frequently repeat these words: "Bless ye the God of heaven, give glory to him in the sight of all that live, because he hath shewn his mercy to you" (Tob. 12:6). Or "Bless the Lord, O my soul: and let all that is within me bless his holy name. Bless the Lord, O my soul, and never forget all he hath done for

---

of Nebuchadnezzar (see Dan. 3:52–90). The canticle is continued in part throughout this meditation.

thee. Who forgiveth all thy iniquities: who healeth all thy diseases" (Ps. 102:1–3).

In the evening, let us address ourselves to the Blessed Virgin as the daughter of the Eternal Father, and let us recite in her honor three Hail Marys to return thanks for the preparation she made for the mystery of the Incarnation, by means of which we have received this Bread of Life as a most useful and efficacious remedy for all our maladies. And certainly, it is very just that we should testify to this Mother of Mercy a gratitude full of tenderness, since we owe to her the Flesh and Blood of Jesus Christ with which we are nourished. His sacred Body was formed in her chaste womb, and if we approach this divine sacrament with fervor and devotion, if we obtain the pardon of our sins, if we increase in virtue and in sanctity, all these graces are the fruit of her prayers and intercession.

Second Day

Let us occupy ourselves in thanksgiving to the Son of God for the benefit of redemption, which is represented to us every day in the Blessed Sacrament. And since in taking on Himself our flesh in His infinite goodness, He has been willing to unite Himself to earth, let us invite all the creatures who are on the earth to join with us in thanking Him, in this manner:

> O let the earth bless the Lord; let it praise and exalt Him above all forever.
>
> O you mountains and hills, bless the Lord; bless the Lord, all things that spring forth on earth.
>
> O you fountains, bless the Lord; bless the Lord, you seas and floods.
>
> O you whales and all that move in the waters, bless the Lord; bless the Lord, all you birds of the air.
>
> O all you beasts and cattle, bless the Lord; bless the Lord, you sons of men.

When reciting these words, we should think of the mountain of Calvary upon which Jesus Christ shed His Blood, that this celestial dew may render the earth of our souls fruitful in good works. Let us bless a thousand times these adorable wounds, the fountains of the Savior of which the prophet Isaiah speaks, from which we should draw saving waters of grace with much joy and consolation. Let us consider that the animals that live in the waters represent our Lord, who lived in the waters of tribulation; and that they are a figure of those holy souls who live, so to speak, in the Blood of our Savior by their constant meditation of His sufferings. Moreover, let us reflect that the birds of the air, which build their nests in the holes in the rocks, are symbolic of those who find their repose in the wounds of Jesus crucified; and finally, that we, the sons of mere men, have become the children of God by the merits of our Redeemer.

In order to stir up our hearts during the day and to excite them to bless the Lord, we should make use of the same aspirations as on the preceding day, or of the following: "Bless the Lord, O my soul, and never forget all He hath done for thee.... Who redeemeth thy life from destruction; who crowneth thee with mercy and compassion" (Ps. 102:2, 4).

In the evening, we should make a visit to the Mother of God and say three Hail Marys to thank her for having nourished with her milk Him who has made Himself our nourishment, and for having given us this Adorable Bread, which was offered on the tree of the Cross and which is still offered every day on the altar, as a propitiatory sacrifice for a remedy for our diseases and the support of our weakness. Let us also thank her for the particular graces we have received in Communion.

Third Day

Let us thank the Holy Spirit for the grace of our adoption, which is renewed so often by Holy Communion. But let us also consider that the bread with which we have been nourished is the bread of the children of God and should not have been given "to the dogs who return to their vomit," to use the words of Scripture (see Prov. 26:11)—that is to say, to those who so easily fall back again into sin. Let us remember that this bread, being received with a pure heart, has the power to increase in us the spirit of adoption that gives us the courage to call God our Father; that this divine sacrament is a sacred fountain in which our souls renew their youth, like the eagle, and recover that beauty and innocence that they had received in Baptism. Thus, we should on this day try to increase our faith and all the virtues we have received in that first sacrament, Baptism, so that we may become new men and true Israelites.

We ought afterward to recite the remainder of the canticle and invite the other creatures to return thanks to the Lord:

> Let Israel bless the Lord; let him praise and exalt Him above all forever.

> O you priests of the Lord, bless the Lord; bless the Lord, you servants of the Lord.
>
> O you spirits and souls of the just, bless the Lord; bless the Lord, all you that are holy and humble of heart.
>
> O Hananiah, Azariah, Mishael,[5] bless the Lord; praise and exalt Him above all forever.
>
> Let us bless the Father, and the Son, and the Holy Spirit; let us praise and exalt Him above all forever.
>
> Blessed are You, O Lord, in the firmament of Heaven, worthy to be praised and glorified and exalted above all forever.

We ought to remember, in offering this adorable Victim to God, to offer ourselves also and to make a sacrifice of our hearts to Him so that we may be of the number of priests who bless Him and of those faithful servants to whom our Lord said, "Enter thou into the joy of thy lord" (Matt. 25:23). For He longs exceedingly to give Himself to us, and His delight is "to be with the children of men" (Prov. 8:31). And since the grace of this divine sacrament

[5] The Hebrew names of Shadrach, Meshach, and Abednego.

makes us true adorers who "adore him in spirit and in truth" (John 4:24), by the union of love, which we have with God, let us apply the words of the canticle in this manner: "Spirits and souls of the just, who have received Him who is our sanctity and our justice, bless the Lord; bless the Lord, you humble of heart, since He has deigned to humble Himself even to our lowliness. May the three powers of our soul bless the Lord as the three children formerly did in the furnace, since He has vouchsafed to descend upon them with the dew of His grace, to deliver the understanding from error and ignorance, the memory from forgetfulness and ingratitude, and the will from coldness and malice. Blessed be the Father, the Son, and the Holy Spirit, for all eternity."

In addition, we should constantly repeat during the day these words to animate our fervor: "Bless the Lord, all his works: in every place of his dominion, O my soul, bless thou the Lord. Who satisfieth thy desire with good things: thy youth shall be renewed like the eagle's" (Ps. 102:22, 5).

In the evening, let us again address ourselves to the Blessed Virgin, who is the spouse of the Holy Spirit, and say three Hail Marys to return her thanks for having offered her well-beloved Son on the Cross to deliver us from death. For if we are grateful to those who employ their riches in drawing us from any danger, what should be our gratitude toward that Mother of Mercy who, in giving her Son for our salvation, has given us her flesh, her blood, her love, her joy, and her only good. Let us return her, then, a thousand acts of thanksgiving for so many favors and for all those that we have received in Holy Communion by her prayers and intercession.

Daily Reflections for Greater Self-Knowledge

Daily Reflections

If we wish to be of the number of those who have not "received their souls in vain," according to the words of the prophet (see Ps. 23:4), we should reflect on what God has done with regard to us and how we have acted with regard to God. The frequent meditation of these two things, by making us know our own weakness and the graces we receive from God, will induce us to love Him with all our strength in this life in order to possess Him for all eternity.

This exercise is divided into seven parts for the seven days of the week. Each part contains: 1. a meditation with a short reflection at the end on one of the mysteries of the life of Jesus Christ; 2. a prayer to God; and 3. some devout aspirations taken from the Holy Scriptures with which to occupy our minds during the day and to rouse our tepidity.

If we make use of this exercise, we will soon experience its advantages. For as it is impossible to draw near the fire without feeling heat, neither can we approach the divine love by meditation without being warmed with its holy flames. Let us then, O devout souls, embrace this practice with ardor; let us do on earth what the seraphim do in Heaven, who cease not to love and glorify God. Amen.

Daily Preparation for Each Exercise

At the start of each daily exercise, prepare your mind, heart, and soul in the following manner:

1. Purify your conscience by an acknowledgment of your sins. Endeavor to feel contrition for them, resolve to confess them, and recite the Lord's Prayer and a Hail Mary in a spirit of penance.
2. Beg Jesus Christ to illuminate your mind with His lights and to inflame your heart with His love.
3. Join to a distrust in yourself an entire confidence in His goodness, since it is certain that, in redeeming the world, He thought of you, had regard to your misery, and prayed to His Father for you.

4. As, according to the testimony of the Apostle, we are incapable of forming of ourselves any good thoughts, "Not that we are sufficient to think any thing of ourselves, as of ourselves: but our sufficiency is from God" (2 Cor. 3:5), say these words: "Come, O Holy Spirit, visit the souls of Thy servants, and fill with Thy holy grace the hearts Thou has created."

Exercises for Specific Days

Monday

Meditation

1. Let me consider what God has done for me: it is He who has created me, it is from Him that I have received being; and instead of gratefully recognizing His benefits, I have trampled them underfoot; I have returned to nothingness by sin; I have lost the life of grace that He had given me; and my hands have destroyed the work of His hands.
2. He was not content with giving me being, He wished to create me in His own image. And I have very frequently despised this divine image, I have corrupted its beauty, and I have taken no care to preserve it.

3. The only recompense He desires for so great a favor is that I allow Him to give Himself to me. But although I know well that what He exacts from me is for my advantage, it appears that the only thing I wish is to fly far from Him and separate myself from Him, as if I could live without Him. Although He knew, in creating me, how ungrateful I should be for this grace, He nevertheless wished to become man so that He might wash out my sins with His Blood.

Finish this meditation by the consideration of the mystery of the Incarnation, and return thanks for it to Jesus Christ.

Prayer

O my God, Creator of Heaven and of earth, make me know all the good Thou has done me by Thy bounty, and all the evil I have done by my malice; that being convinced I have destroyed in myself what Thou has built up, and have effaced all the traces of Thine image, I may declare a continual war against myself until Thy grace binds me in such manner to Thee that I can no more offend Thee. Thou will then do all things in me, according to Thy promise, "Let not the foot of pride come to me, and let not the hand of the sinner move me" (Ps. 35:12), and Thou will be eternally glorified in Thy work. Amen.

Aspiration

Perditio tua, Israel: tantummodo in Me auxilium tuum.

"Destruction is thy own, O Israel: thy help is only in me" (Hos. 13:9).

TUESDAY

Meditation

1. Let me consider that God has formed me out of earth and dust, so that I might always have before my eyes the lowness of my origin and never lose the remembrance of my being weak and subject to death. Nevertheless, instead of occupying myself with so saving a thought, I have always kept my mind from it and have lived as if I were never to die.
2. God has given me a body subject to a thousand infirmities, full of corruption and putrefaction, in order that I should not be attached to it; and, nevertheless, I have labored for it alone, I have treated it with extreme delicacy, without considering that it must become the food of worms.
3. God has wished that my soul should be immortal and incorruptible and that after death my body should become the most horrible and insupportable thing in the world, in order that I might not study the well-being

of my body in comparison with that of my soul. And I, by a strange perversity, have neglected this soul that should be so dear to me, and this corruptible flesh has been the only object of my care and tenderness.

Our Lord did not abhor to take on Himself our body, all miserable as it is, and to be born in poverty. Let me finish this meditation by the consideration of the mystery of the birth of my Savior, and by thanking Him for having emptied Himself out for our love.

Prayer

"Lord, what is man that thou shouldst magnify him? or why dost thou set thy heart upon him?" (see Job 7:17).

Since we have failed in gratitude for Thy favors through ignorance of our own misery, may we at least acknowledge that we have allowed ourselves to be surprised by pride and a vain esteem of ourselves.

I ask Thee, then, O my God, to enlighten my spirit and to inspire me with sentiments of sincere humility, so that, after the example of holy Job, I may say to the dust, "Thou art my father; to worms, my mother and my sister" (Job 17:14), that thus I may be convinced I can do nothing without Thee, that Thou are my only refuge and my sovereign good.

Receive me, then, O Lord. I give myself entirely to Thee; do not reject the work of Thy hands; make me so that I can say with truth: "My father and my mother have left me; but the Lord hath taken me up" (Ps. 26:10); may He be blessed and glorified forever and ever. Amen.

Aspiration

Qui quasi putredo consumendus sum, et quasi vestimentum quod comeditur a tinea.

"Who am to be consumed as rottenness, and as a garment that is moth-eaten" (Job 13:28).

WEDNESDAY

Meditation

1. God has wished to enrich my soul with three faculties. First, He has given me memory so that I might never forget His favors and might be consoled with the remembrance of His goodness. But alas! I have occupied this memory with other things. What confusion for me to have filled it with so many useless and criminal thoughts, which have sullied the purity of my soul and extinguished in it the grace of my God.
2. God has given me understanding to know the truth and to contemplate His infinite perfections. But I have

darkened it by the false maxims of the world and the flesh. I have rebelled against the light and can truly say with the prophet David, "For evils without number have surrounded me; my iniquities have overtaken me, and I was not able to see" (Ps. 39:13).

3. He has given me a will capable of tasting in this life the sweetness of divine love and of obtaining, by the good use of my liberty and by the merits of Jesus Christ, the grace of loving Him for all eternity. But alas! This will is attached to creatures who have caused it only disgust and bitterness. I have abused my liberty, and, child of God that I was, I have become a slave of the devil.

I have been unwilling to regulate the faculties of my soul or to cut off what was displeasing in them to Jesus Christ, and He has been willing to be circumcised and shed His Blood for love of me, eight days after His birth. Let me conclude this meditation by the thought of this mystery.

Prayer

Lord, what has so enchanted my memory, amidst the perishable things of earth, as to give them a place that is due to Thee alone? Has my understanding found anything that deserves its application? And my will, has it been able to meet outside of Thee an object worthy of its love? All that these love except Thyself, O my God, cause much more grief than joy. But since my mind has become darkened and I have fallen into forgetfulness of Thy mercies by the perversity of my will, shed for the future so much bitterness over all earthly pleasures that I may love Thee alone, who desires to be the object of my love. Amen.

Aspiration

Et posuerunt adversum me mala pro bonis: et odium pro dilectione mea.

"And they repaid me evil for good: and hatred for my love" (Ps. 108:5).

THURSDAY

Meditation

1. God has given me eyes so I may recognize His perfections in those of creatures, and so all I see may draw me to love and glorify my Creator. But I have made use of these eyes to draw His enemies into my soul, and I have used those creatures even against the Being who had given them to me.
2. He has given me the sense of smell so I may enjoy the perfume of flowers, so I may glorify Him in them, and,

like the spouse in the Song of Solomon, run after the odor of His perfumes (see 1:3). But I have used it only to please myself, and I have said with the sinners, "Let us crown ourselves with roses, before they be withered" (Wisd. 2:8).

3. He has given me ears so I may hear the voice of the Spouse and so my soul may be comforted; but I have closed them to His holy inspirations and opened them to slander.
4. He has given me with much liberality a great abundance of all kinds of food for my nourishment; and instead of being grateful for His bounty, and instead of tasting interiorly how sweet is the Lord, I have changed His benefits into poison, I have lost the relish for holy things; the Manna of Heaven has appeared insipid to me, and I have sought with eagerness the nourishment of sinners.
5. He has given me hands to do good works, which should rejoice the angels and merit Paradise; and I have done only wicked actions, which have afflicted the good and have rendered me worthy of the pains of Hell.

Jesus Christ was led by the Holy Spirit into the desert, to expiate, by a fast of forty days, the sins that I have committed by my appetite. The consideration of this mystery will end this meditation.

Prayer

What shall I say, O Lord, of these eyes, which, like two fatal torches, have enkindled in my heart the fire of concupiscence by the sight of creatures instead of inflaming it with Thy love? What shall I say of my ears, which have been deaf to the groans of those in distress? What use have I made of my tongue? How many times have I allowed myself to be surprised by the deceitful allurements of things that appeal to the senses? What shall I say of the works of my hands, and what shall I make answer to Thee, O Lord, since I have so misused them? Where shall I seek help? For although I have fallen through my own weakness, I cannot rise again by my own strength alone, and I can well say with the prophet, "My heart is troubled, my strength hath left me" (Ps. 37:11). Thou alone, then, O my God, are my refuge and my hope; from Thy goodness alone do I expect my help and my cure. Make my senses submissive to Thy holy will, so that they may become instruments of Thy glory. Amen.

Aspiration

Quia ascendit mors per fenestras nostras.... Non ambuletis sicut et gentes ambulant in vanitate sensus sui.

"For death is come up through our windows.... Walk not as also the Gentiles walk in the vanity of their mind" (Jer. 9:21; Eph. 4:17).

FRIDAY

Meditation

1. God did not deprive me of the use of creatures after my sin, He has even preserved in me the life and strength that I have used to offend Him; and I, instead of recognizing myself unworthy of the creatures I have used so badly, I complain and murmur when I want for anything; I have wished for life and strength only to follow with more liberty my unruly desires.
2. He has protected me against my enemies, visible and invisible, and He has marked me with His seal, as He formerly did to Cain for fear that the demons would avenge the injury he had done to God. And I have sought the enemies I should have fled from, and I have abandoned myself, in sinning, to those who have conspired my ruin.

3. He has given me friends to warn me, preachers to threaten me, angels to instruct me, and the death of my neighbors to awaken me from my dangerous sloth; finally, He has offered me graces that I could never deserve. But I have closed my ears to the counsels of my friends; my heart has been obdurate to menaces and inspirations; I have kept my mind from the thought of death, to obey those who wished my ruin, and I have abandoned my God who has died to save me.

Reflect on what Jesus Christ has suffered for your salvation, and finish this meditation by the thought of His death and His passion.

Prayer

What have I found in Thee, Lord, to make me persecute Thee? And what have I found in myself to love with so much passion? What can Thou expect from me that Thou has so patiently borne with me? And what good can I expect for myself in offending Thee? Yes, my God, I recognize now Thy infinite goodness, and I implore Thee that this goodness may force me at length to love Thee and bind me forever to Thy service, so that I may be as much Thine by grace as I am Thine by creation. Amen.

Aspiration

Quid est quod debui ultra facere vineae meae, et non feci ei? An quod expectavi ut faceret uvas, et fecit labruscas?

"What is there that I ought to do more to my vineyard that I have not done to it? Was it that I looked that it should bring forth grapes, and it hath brought forth wild grapes?" (Isa. 5:4).[6]

Saturday

Meditation

1. If God had treated me with the severity I deserved, where should I now be? My memory, for having forgotten my Creator, should have been punished in Hell by the eternal remorse that this forgetfulness would cause me. My understanding should have known in the midst of those inextinguishable flames what to have done to avoid them; and my will would have been penetrated with an undying grief for being obliged to suffer such horrible torments during all eternity as a punishment for having refused to bear light ones in this life. But if I had done with regard to God what

[6] The second sentence in this passage is missing from the Douay-Rheims, but it is present in the Vulgate.

I ought to have done, I should have feared above all things to fall into forgetfulness of His goodness. My mind should have been applied only to the things that regard His glory and His service, and my heart should have been inflamed with His love. But alas! I am so miserable that instead of expiating my past crimes, I commit new ones every day and procure for myself additional pains.

2. If God had treated me as I deserved, my eyes would have been punished with horrible darkness and by the continued sight of the devils. My ears would have heard nothing but the cries of the damned. I would have smelled only an insupportable stench. I should have tasted only the bitter chalice of all sorts of torments, and I should have touched flames alone. But if I had done what I ought, I should not have avoided with so much care disagreeable objects, outrages, calumnies, bad odors, and things bitter to the taste, nor even the fire of this world, if it were necessary to suffer it to escape that of Hell. But alas! Senseless that I was, I preferred to avoid the trials of this life than to deliver myself, by suffering them, from eternal pains.
3. God has preserved me from sin, and consequently from Hell, from which He delivers me each moment

by the preservation of His grace. How many times has He prevented me from being lost? How many times has He restored me to grace when I had ruined myself? Should I not, after so many favors, sing eternally the mercies of the Lord and bind myself to Him, never to be separated? But alas! I try to break the chains of His charity in order to take part with His enemies and to throw myself more freely into the precipice.

Consider that Jesus descended into Hell to draw from it the holy fathers of the Old Testament, and that His Body remained attached to the Cross, at the foot of which was His holy Mother.

Prayer

Lord, I can say rightly with the prophet, "My soul is filled with evils; and my life hath drawn nigh to hell" (Ps. 87:4). For how many times has Thou drawn me, O my God, from the shades of death, when I should have been lost eternally? But since it is true that all coming from me leads to death, and that all coming from Thyself gives life, I implore Thee, make me know myself in order to hate myself, and make me know Thee that I may love Thee with all my heart and give myself entirely to Thee, who has created and delivered me from death by Thy mercy. Amen.

Aspiration

Nisi quia Dominus adjuvit me: paulominus habitasset in inferno anima mea.

"Unless the Lord had been my helper, my soul had almost dwelt in hell" (Ps. 93:17).

SUNDAY

Meditation

1. God is always with me; it is from Him I have life, movement, and being; He guards me while I sleep; He never abandons me. I should therefore unceasingly pay Him the profoundest respect, as He is so near me, and I should always love Him, since He never leaves me. But alas! I do not cease to offend Him, although He is continually loading me with favors.
2. He is not ignorant of my crimes, since He knows all things, and He offers me a remedy for them. But I am so perverse that, instead of making use of them, I give myself up to my unruly desires.
3. He disposes all things with kindness and waits a favorable opportunity for producing virtues in my soul. But

I destroy in a moment what He has set up in so long a time and with such unfailing patience.

4. He inspires me with sentiments of humility and self-confusion for fear that I may corrupt by my pride the graces with which He has enriched my soul. But alas! If I have not entirely plucked up these divine seeds, it is at least certain that I have allowed them to wither, and that I have choked them so much by the cares and pleasures of this life that it is difficult for them to produce any fruit.
5. While I am in a state of grace, God unites Himself to me by charity, He nourishes and increases this divine virtue in my soul by the adorable sacrament of the Eucharist. Finally, He gives Himself to me in all kinds of ways, and the only thing He asks of me is that I be willing to receive Him. And I separate myself every moment from Him. I refuse the Bread of Angels that He offers me, and it appears as if I were resolved to oppose myself to all the good He wishes to do me.

Let me think of the Resurrection of my Savior and how much I owe to the Eternal Father for having rendered so glorious the wounds that I have inflicted on His only Son. Let me consider that He is seated at the right hand of His

Father and that He is honored by good works, but that His judgment will be terrible for those who have dishonored Him by their wicked actions.

Prayer

O abyss of divine wisdom! I will repeat with the Psalmist, "Lord, thy way is in the sea, and thy paths in many waters: and thy footsteps shall not be known" (see Ps. 76:20). I ought to be overwhelmed with astonishment when I feel within me any good desire, and much more so when I execute it. How can I dare hope that Thou wish to sow the seed of Thy graces in such sterile soil, or that it could produce any fruit? Were I fully convinced that I choke this divine seed, that I trample it underfoot when it commences to shoot upward, and that I scatter the fruit it produces, I should be obliged to humble myself in all things; and even the good Thou work in me would fill me with humility. Grant, then, O my God, in Thy mercy, that I may know my misery, and that I may glorify Thy holy name for all eternity. Amen.

Aspiration

Mecum eras, et tecum non eram. . . . sero te amavi, pulchritudo tam antiqua et tam nova, sero te amavi!

"You were with me, but I was not with You. . . . Too late did I love You, O Fairness, so ancient, and yet so new! Too late did I love You!" (St. Augustine, *Confessions* 10.27.38).[7]

[7] Latin text available at "Augustini Confessionum Liber Decimus," *The Latin Library*, www.thelatinlibrary.com/augustine/conf10.shtml; English translation is from *Nicene and Post-Nicene Fathers*, first series, vol. 1, trans. J. G. Pilkington, ed. Philip Schaff (Buffalo, NY: Christian Literature Publishing, 1887), rev. and ed. for New Advent by Kevin Knight, www.newadvent.org/fathers/110110.htm.

Biography of St. Francis Borgia, Confessor

St. Francis Borgia, fourth Duke of Gandia and third General of the Jesuits, was the son of John Borgia, Duke of Gandia and Grandee of Spain, and of Joanna of Aragon. The family of Borgia (or Berja) had long flourished in Spain, but they had received a new luster by the exaltation of Cardinal Alfonso Borgia to the Pontificate, under the name of Calixtus III, in 1455. St. Francis was born in 1510, at Gandia, a town that was the chief seat of the family, in the kingdom of Valencia. As soon as he was capable of speaking, his parents taught him to pronounce the holy names of Jesus and Mary, and at five years of age, he recited daily on his knees the chief part of the catechism. When he was ten years old, he had the misfortune to lose his pious mother, Joanna of Aragon. This event had a great effect on him and seemed to deepen his religious impressions. Owing to his exalted station, he was obliged to mix with worldly men, but in his intercourse with them, he never suffered himself to be drawn aside into any excesses or even laxity of demeanor.

The death of the pious Empress Isabella happened on May 1, 1539.[8] When the funeral convoy arrived at Gandia and her corpse was delivered into the hands of the magistrates of that city, both sides were to make oath that it was the body of the empress. The coffin of lead was therefore opened and her face uncovered, but it appeared so hideous and disfigured that no one knew it. St. Francis, being exceedingly struck by this spectacle, exclaimed, "What is now become of those eyes once so sparkling? Where is now the beauty and graceful air of that countenance which we so lately beheld? Art thou Donna Isabella, her revered majesty? Art thou my empress and my lady, my mistress?" The impression made on his soul

[8] Isabella of Portugal (1503–1539), wife and empress consort of Holy Roman Emperor and Spanish King Charles V. She held many roles during her life, including regent of Spain whenever her husband was away.

by this spectacle remained burned into his mind during the remainder of his life.

In obedience to the wish of the Emperor Charles V, he married Eleanor de Castro, a noble lady of exemplary piety. He filled several of the highest offices of state with so much prudence and probity as to win the admiration of all classes with whom he was brought into contact, living meanwhile in the practice of the severest austerities. He constantly wore a hair shirt and put small stones in his shoes; during two successive Lents he took nothing but leeks and garlic for his one meal, and afterward, he continued this practice for a whole year. His wife being sick unto death, he would not pray for her recovery but made a vow that if she died, he would become a Jesuit. Indeed, when she died, he fulfilled his vow and entered the Society of Jesus, and on July 2, 1565, he was chosen to be Third General of the Order. He finished a holy life by a more holy and edifying death, and he closed his eyes upon the world on September 30, 1572.

Sophia Institute

Sophia Institute is a nonprofit institution that seeks to nurture the spiritual, moral, and cultural life of souls and to spread the gospel of Christ in conformity with the authentic teachings of the Roman Catholic Church.

Sophia Institute Press fulfills this mission by offering translations, reprints, and new publications that afford readers a rich source of the enduring wisdom of mankind.

Sophia Institute also operates the popular online resource CatholicExchange.com. *Catholic Exchange* provides world news from a Catholic perspective as well as daily devotionals and articles that will help readers to grow in holiness and live a life consistent with the teachings of the Church.

In 2013, Sophia Institute launched Sophia Institute for Teachers to renew and rebuild Catholic culture through service to Catholic education. With the goal of nurturing the spiritual, moral, and cultural life of souls, and an abiding respect for the role and work of teachers, we strive to provide materials and programs that are at once enlightening to the mind and ennobling to the heart; faithful and complete, as well as useful and practical.

Sophia Institute gratefully recognizes the Solidarity Association for preserving and encouraging the growth of our apostolate over the course of many years. Without their generous and timely support, this book would not be in your hands.

www.SophiaInstitute.com
www.CatholicExchange.com
www.SophiaInstituteforTeachers.org